MASTER THIS!

Street Dance

Emma Torrington

PowerKiDS
press.

New York

Published in 2012 by The Rosen Publishing Group Inc.
29 East 21st Street, New York, NY 10010

First Edition

Series Editor: Rasha Elsaaed
Editor: Julia Adams

Produced by Tall Tree Ltd
Editor, Tall Tree: Neil Kelly
Designer: Jonathan Vipond

Library of Congress Cataloging-in-Publication Data

Torrington, Emma.
Street dance / by Emma Torrington. -- 1st ed.
    p. cm. -- (Master this!)
Includes index.
ISBN 978-1-4488-5285-7 (library binding)
1. Dance--Juvenile literature. 2. Break dancing--Juvenile
literature. 3. Hip-hop dance--Juvenile literature. I. Title.
GV1596.5.T67 2012
793.3--dc22

                                      2010046330

Manufactured in China
CPSIA Compliance Information: Batch # WAS1102PK: For Further Information
contact Rosen Publishing, New York, New York at 1-800-237-9932

Photographs
All photographs taken by Michael Wicks, except;
t-top, b-bottom, l-left, r-right, c-center
4l Poweron, 5 Dreamstime.com/Dmytro Konstantynov,
25tr Jen Keys, 29 JMEnternational/Redferns.Getty

Disclaimer

In preparation of this book, all due care has been
exercised with regard to the advice, activities, and
techniques depicted. The publishers regret that they
can accept no liability for any loss or injury sustained.
When learning a new skill, it is important to get expert
instruction and to follow a manufacturer's guidelines.

Contents

What Is Street Dance?

Street dance is an energetic, vibrant dance form. It mixes together moves that originated in street styles, such as **breaking**, with established forms such as **jazz, tap,** and **salsa**.

Jazz Origins

The roots of street dance can be traced back to the 1920s and 1930s, when jazz and tap dancers figured out dance moves inspired by the beats and rhythm of jazz music. In the 1970s, new dance styles, including **popping** and **locking** (see page 10), were developed around **funk music** rhythms. By the end of the 1970s, **DJs** had created a new musical style—**hip-hop**. Groups of dancers created moves and styles, such as **freezes** and **power moves** (see pages 20–21) to suit this new music.

Teams of street dancers, called crews, often perform impressive moves, such as handstands and leg spins.

Star File

BOOGALOO SAM
Popping Pioneer

The set of movements we know as popping was developed by "Boogaloo" Sam Solomon, founder of 1970s' funk dance group, The Electric Boogaloos. The technique got its name because Sam would say "pop, pop, pop" under his breath as he popped his muscles while performing the moves.

Top Tip

Fast, upbeat music is ideal for working on your street dancing techniques. It is a good idea to practice your moves to your favorite music, so that you are familiar with the rhythm.

Practicing your street dancing moves is a fun way to keep fit and will improve your body's flexibility.

Street Dance Today

The great thing about street dance is that it is still developing today, as modern musical influences, such as **R & B** music and Latin-American rhythms, inspire new dance moves. It is a dance form that anyone can master—you can create your own moves and could even end up having a move named after you. Street dance is also great exercise. It can help to improve fitness, build strength, and improve coordination.

Diet

Dancing involves a lot of exercise, so eating the right food is vital to keep your body in top shape. Energy-rich foods, such as whole-grain pasta and rice, will help you to dance for long periods. Fish, lean meat, eggs, and beans provide protein to maintain your muscles. Foods that are sources of healthy fats, such as seeds, nuts, and olive oil, will help to keep your heart healthy.

Clothing and Accessories

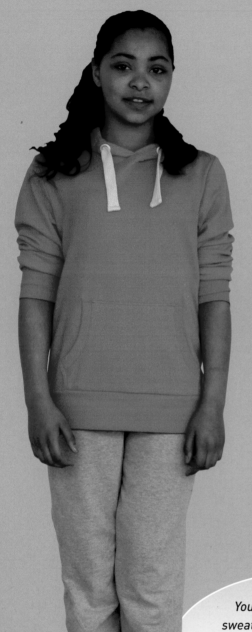

Although there is no strict uniform for street dance, you need to wear clothing that is comfortable and does not restrict your movements. Make sure that your knees are covered for moves that involve a lot of kneeling and sliding on the floor.

What to Wear

An important part of street dance is to express yourself through movement. Think of your clothing as a costume to help convey your own personality and style. Once you have mastered the basics, you may want to try more advanced moves. For these, you will need knee pads, which are essential for protecting your joints during power moves (see pages 20–21).

Your clothing should take sweat away from your body as you dance. Sneakers should have white or pale soles so that they do not mark the dance studio's floor.

Knee pads

Dance studios have large, wall-to-wall mirrors. These can help dancers when they are working on their performance skills.

Dance Studios

Street dance is designed to be performed anywhere, but the best place to practice moves is in a studio. A studio will have a sprung floor, which will help protect your back and knees from injury by acting as a shock absorber. It will also help you get better elevation (height) for jumps and acrobatic moves. A mirror will enable you to check that you are performing your moves properly.

Top Tip

You will improve your dance skills more quickly with the use of a mirror, but do not become too dependent on it. When you are dancing, try to perform to an invisible audience "beyond" the mirror.

Conditioning and Practice

Street dancing can be physically demanding. These warm-up and conditioning exercises will help you get your whole body in shape. Do not forget to work on the hands, which take your full body weight during floor work, and try to maintain a good posture.

Stretching all of your muscles prevents injuries. Here, dancers are stretching their leg muscles. Ask your teacher how to perform stretches correctly.

Warm-up Exercises

A warm-up should start off with some light exercise, such as jogging. This will raise your heart rate so that more blood flows to your muscles, allowing them to work harder and for longer. You can then move on to some stretches to prepare your joints and muscles for the class ahead. Over time, stretching muscles will also make them more supple, allowing you to perform more extreme moves.

Posture and Weight

When you dance, keep your back straight, pull in your stomach muscles, and keep your shoulders down. Let your arms hang by your sides, with your head facing forward. Keep your weight forward on your toes—this will stop you from falling over.

Conditioning Exercises

Practicing these conditioning exercises will strengthen the muscle groups used in dancing. Sit-ups tone your stomach muscles and the core muscles around your back and trunk, and pushups help to develop upper body strength. Handstands develop the arms, wrists, and hands to help with floor work and power moves.

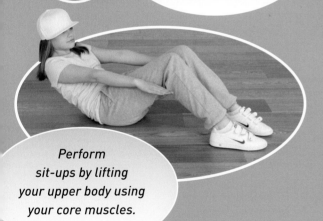

Practice your handstands against a wall to stop yourself falling down.

Perform sit-ups by lifting your upper body using your core muscles.

Use your upper body muscles in pushups to push yourself off the floor.

To perform the warm-ups and conditioning exercises, as well as the dance moves you are going to learn, you will need to master these essential feet positions.

In the parallel first position, the feet are positioned parallel to each other, facing forward about 4 inches (10 cm) apart.

In the parallel second position, the feet should be shoulder-width apart.

In the parallel fourth position, the feet should be parallel with each other with one foot placed in front.

9

Essential Moves

Locking, popping, and spins are essential street dance moves. Locking and popping feature controlled hand and arm movements. Spins require good balance and coordination.

Locking and Popping

Locking features fast, distinct hand and arm movements that finish in a frozen "locked" moment. You need to quickly tense and relax your muscles to do this. Popping moves, where a dancer releases or "pops" out a part of the body, are smaller than locking moves, as you tense and relax a specific body part to create sharp, controlled movements.

Popping

This dancer starts a popping move by relaxing his arms and hands.

He then pops his hands into place, by tensing his elbows and wrists.

Locking

A simple locking move sees this dancer moving his upper body from side to side, locking the body rigid.

When locking from side to side, keep your fingers straight and thumbs tucked into your palms.

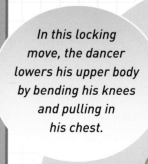

In this locking move, the dancer lowers his upper body by bending his knees and pulling in his chest.

Basic Spin

1

To start a basic spin, this dancer has placed her right foot across and in front of her body.

2

She pushes off with her right foot and spins around on her left, until she has completed a full spin.

3

When she has completed the spin, her left foot will be across her body with her arms held out for balance.

Spinning Around

Spins, or pirouettes, are impressive moves that require control, coordination, balance, and strong leg muscles. Different spins are used in floor moves and can be incorporated into solo and group street dance routines. When spinning, keep your head facing forward as your body moves. Snap your head around at the last minute as you complete the spin. This is called spotting. Some spins involve movements in mid-air. To perform a tuck spin, jump in the air, tuck your knees into your body, and twist from the waist to spin your body around.

In this pirouette, the right knee is bent while spinning.

Isolation Techniques

Isolation techniques take the movements used in popping and locking (see page 10) a step further. They use short, quick muscle contractions to create robotic movements isolated to one area, while the rest of the body remains motionless. Isolation techniques are the building blocks for more complicated moves.

Rib Isolation

In isolation techniques, any movement starts near the center of the body, moves out to the farthest point, and then returns toward the center. Rib isolation involves shifting the rib cage to the left, right, backward, and forward, without moving other parts of the body. The ribs are concave, or pushed inward, during these exercises, with the shoulders relaxed and "floating" on top.

Rib Isolation Moves

1. Keeping his waist and legs still, the dancer moves his rib cage over to his right.

2. He then moves his ribs back to the middle, before moving them to his left.

3. Returning to the middle, he then pushes his ribs out in front of him.

4. In the final part of the move, he pulls his ribs and stomach in.

Hip Isolation

During a hip isolation move, the hips move to the right, the center, forward, to the left, and backward, while everything above the waist is kept still. This exercise is an essential technique for performing the body **ripple** (see pages 16–17). You can also alter both the hip and rib isolation exercises. For example, after moving to the right in the rib isolation, you can try moving to the back rather than the front.

Try the rib isolation with your arms held in a low "V" position (see right). Then try the "V" position in a hip isolation move.

Hip Isolation Moves

1

Here the dancer starts off the hip isolation by moving her hips to her right.

2

She moves her hips back to the middle before pushing them out to her left.

3

Returning to the middle, she then pushes her hips backward.

4

In the final part of the move, she pushes her hips forward.

13

Rotation Techniques

In **rotation techniques,** a body part moves around in a circular, isolated movement, instead of from side to side as with isolation techniques. The rotation movement is smooth, continuous, and even.

Rib Rotation

In this move, the ribs are isolated and rotate in a circular motion around the body. The rest of the body below the waist is kept motionless as the rib cage is shifted around. This sequence is then repeated in the opposite direction, beginning with a move to the right.

Rib Rotation Technique

1

To start a rib rotation, this dancer has pushed his rib cage out to his left.

2

Without moving back to the center, he pushes his ribs back and around.

3

He continues the move by pushing his ribs around to his right.

4

To complete the rotation, he moves his ribs around the front and then back to his left.

Star File

CRAZY LEGS
Power Moves
Innovator

Richard "Crazy Legs" Colón pioneered power moves in the 1980s. He is best known for the "continuous back" move, in which the dancer spins on his upper back with the assistance of his elbow. He is the president of the Rock Steady Crew, who brought breaking to Europe in 1983.

Hip Rotation

Here, the hips are tilted and rotated in a circular motion around the center of the dancer's body. The knees are bent while performing the moves, and the hands rest on the thighs. As in the hip isolation exercise, the body does not move above the waist.

Hip Rotation Technique

This dancer begins a hip rotation by pushing her hips forward.

She then rotates her hips to her left, keeping the rest of her body still.

Next, the dancer pushes her hips around to the back.

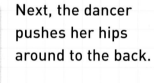

To complete the move, she pushes her hips around to her right and then forward.

Ripple Techniques

The ripple is a fluid, continuous, "rippling" movement of the whole body. It uses both isolation and rotation techniques (see page 12–15). Rippling the body starts by isolating the chest forward and finishes in a forward hip isolation.

Diagonal Ripple

Here, one foot is positioned in front of the other, with the body aligned diagonally. The ribs are isolated and lifted up in a curve. The knees are then bent, and the dancer tilts his or her hips forward, creating a rippling effect.

Diagonal Ripple

To start the ripple, the dancer pushes her chest out while pushing her weight onto her front foot.

She then pulls her chest back, while at the same time pushing her hips forward.

As she pulls her weight back onto her rear foot, she sits back on her hips.

To complete the ripple, her weight is on her rear foot and she stands upright.

Side Ripple

This ripple uses a side to side movement, instead of the forward and back movement used in the diagonal ripple. It uses elements of hip and rib isolation techniques, combining them to create a smooth, flowing ripple.

1

2

The dancer starts by tilting her head to her left.

She then pushes her shoulders to her left.

3

4

To complete the ripple, she moves her head upright and pushes her shoulders back to the middle, before starting the move again.

She then tilts her head and pushes her shoulders to the right.

Changing Direction

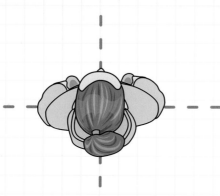

Try moving in different directions and along diagonals. Imagine that you are standing in the middle of a giant cross painted on the floor. The lines of the cross point to the front, back, left, and right of you. If you turn 45 degrees to your right (halfway between the front-facing and right-hand line), you will face the front right diagonal. You can face and travel in this or any other direction on the cross while you dance.

Traveling and Linking

Once you have mastered techniques that are performed in one spot, it is time to get moving around. These simple "traveling" exercises will help improve the quality of your movements and teach you how to transfer your weight while dancing.

Box Step

The **box step** is a great traveling exercise since you will learn to move forward, backward, and to the left and right in a boxlike pattern, shifting your weight smoothly. It will help you learn how to transfer your weight while you dance.

Box Step Techniques

To start a box step, this dancer takes a step forward with her right foot. She then brings her left foot forward as well.

Her next step is to the side, with her right foot leading the way and her left foot following.

She then steps back with her left foot, before bringing her right foot back.

To complete the move, she steps back to her original position with her left foot and then pulls her right foot across.

Rocking Step

The rocking step is a great way to link various moves, including linking standing moves with floor moves (see pages 20–21). It involves springing forward and backward onto the left diagonal with the right foot, and then repeating on the right diagonal with the left foot.

Using arm swings with the box step will add energy to your routine.

Adding Movements

Once you have worked on your foot coordination, try to get your arms moving, too. Swinging the arms will help to give you momentum and add style to your moves. Try sliding the feet, rather then stepping. You could also try jumping the step. Finally, attempt the exercise in double time (twice as fast). Remember, this is a traveling step so make each step big.

Rocking Step

Step out to the left diagonal with your right foot.

Now step back to the middle, swinging your arms up.

Step to the right diagonal with your left foot.

Floor Work

Moving from your feet to the floor brings in a whole new range of dance moves and possibilities. Floor work often entails using your hands, wrists, and arms to take your body weight. For this reason, it is important to have warmed up and conditioned the right body parts to prevent injuries.

Freeze Preparation

The freeze technique involves moving the body and then halting all movement, as if the body has suddenly become frozen in ice. It takes a lot of practice and you need to have good upper body strength to perform it with confidence. The move is used by dancers to add emphasis to beats and to end routines. The freeze preparation exercise (shown right) takes you from a crouching "prayer" position into a handstand, where your arms will take your body weight.

Preparation Exercise

1. This dancer has placed her feet shoulder-width apart and put her elbows inside her knees.

2. She then leans forward, putting her hands on the floor to support her weight.

3. With her weight on her hands, she lifts her feet and slowly places her head on the floor to support her.

The Full Freeze

1

This dancer has placed his right knee in front of his left and tucked his elbows into his body. Most of his weight will be supported by his right arm.

2

He then leans forward, places his head on the floor, and lifts his feet (2), completing the move in the frozen position (3).

3

Performing the Freeze

An actual freeze performance requires more strength than the preparation exercise, because you will hold most of your body weight on one arm, with the other arm just for support. This involves moving from a kneeling position, to supporting your weight on one arm, then finishing in a frozen position with your legs lifted off the floor.

Power Moves

These are acrobatic moves that usually consist of circular motions, where dancers spin on the floor, twirling their legs in the air. The swipe (1), headspin (2), and windmill (3) are three of the best-known power moves.

1

2

3

Creating a Routine

Planning dance routines is called **choreography**. By combining standing techniques with traveling moves, floor work, and directional changes, you can create your own interesting and varied street dance routines.

Routine Preparation

In the solo routine below, thoroughly memorize each set before moving on to the next one. Some parts will seem a little fast, but do not rush them. Try to be really precise, perfecting your moves one step at a time.

Solo Routine

This routine puts together popping, locking, sidesteps, isolations, rotations, freezes, and many of the other moves you have learned.

These moves have been combined to create a 32-count sequence, and this has been broken down into four sets of eight counts.

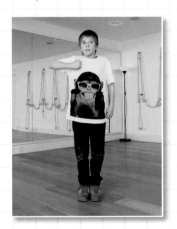

First Set

Walk forward to the count of "1 and 2 and 3 and 4," popping your arms as you move. Bring the left hand to the chest, and on the count of "5," lock it above you, then drop it. Repeat with the right arm for the count of "and 6." Sidestep and return on "7 and 8."

Second Set

Isolate the ribs to the right and left on counts "1" and "2." On "3" and "4," rotate the rib cage in a full circle. On "5," pop both arms out to the right. On "6," turn to the left diagonal and pop both arms in front of you. For "7" and "8," do a body ripple facing the left diagonal.

Planning a Routine

A good starting point when planning a routine is to choose a piece of music. Pick one of your favorite tunes, so that you are familiar with its pace and rhythm—see whether it has eight beats or six. Although many dancers rely on their memory to remember a routine, it is a good idea to make notes, so that you know what is coming next. You can also add simple techniques to enhance your routine, such as claps and kicks.

Take a notepad with you to the dance studio to help you plan your choreography routines.

Third Set

Freestyle for the next count of eight—that means that you can improvise. You could use locking and popping (above left), spins (above right), ripples, stepping, sliding, freezes, or any combination of these moves.

Fourth Set

For the next count of eight, perform the rocking step until the count of "7," starting on the right foot. On "7" make a big step. On the "and" after "7," slide the right knee onto the floor. Transfer your weight through to your hands and move into a freeze on the "8" count.

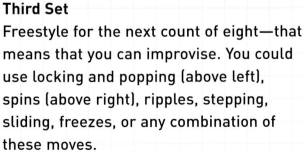
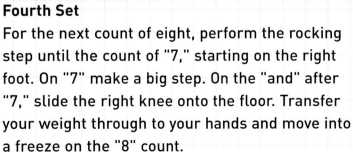

Dancing in Groups

Solo routines can be adapted to work as exciting sequences for many individuals, or separate groups. With more than one dancer on the floor, you can use techniques that enable the dancers to complement each other's moves.

Moving in Unison

Unison is a technique in which all the dancers perform identical movements in time with each other. This creates a dramatic effect, magnifying the visual impact of the moves.

Unison is very effective in group dance routines. By performing the same moves at the same time, it creates the impression that the dancers are acting as one.

24

Mirror Image

In the **mirroring** technique, groups of dancers mirror each other's moves. In a dance sequence featuring two groups, all the dancers move in unison, but one group starts on the opposite foot to begin the set of movements.

Star File

BEYONCÉ
Street-Dancing Pop Star

Beyoncé Knowles (born September 4, 1981) is a world-famous American R & B singer, songwriter, dancer, and actress. The dance choreography she uses in her videos and concerts combines street dancing, hip-hop, and jazz dance influences.

In this mirroring sequence, two groups of dancers are performing reversed, mirror-image versions of each other's moves.

One after the Other

The **canon** technique is a variation on the unison idea. The dancers perform the same moves, but each dancer in the group moves one after the other. This creates a cascading, "domino" or wave effect.

Here, the dancers perform identical movements in sequence, working from left to right across the group.

25

Putting It Together

Combining various group moves can transform a dance routine into a vibrant and energetic display that will leave your audience gasping. Make sure you arrange your dancers and routines so that they produce the maximum impact.

Patterns

These dancers are standing in a V-shape, with the point of the "V" facing the audience. You could also try arranging your dancers in one or two lines.

Create an exciting opening by placing your dancers in a circle so that they launch into their moves while facing in the same direction.

Dance Patterns

Think about the patterns the dancers will move in, such as parallel lines, diagonals, circles, and V-shapes. Incorporate directional, or "orientation" changes in the routines to add interest. If you have a story, or narrative, to tell, show this through your moves and sequences. As with all routines, begin by choosing a piece of your favorite music for inspiration.

Group Routine

By introducing group dance ideas, we can take the 32-count solo routine from pages 22–23 and turn it into a dance for eight people. Split the group into two groups of four (see below). Group one is on the right, group two is on the left. Each dancer uses group dance ideas (see page 24–25) in response to the other dancers', or groups', moves.

Top Tip

Changing direction, or facing a different direction in relation to the moves of other dancers or groups, can add style and excitement to the sequences of a group routine.

Group Routine

The first set of eight counts in this group routine can be performed using mirror techniques.

Try using a unison technique for all eight counts of the second set.

Now the dancers are performing the third set of eight counts using the canon technique to create a domino effect.

To finish the routine with a flourish, the two groups end the final set facing in opposite directions.

Taking It Further

If you want to learn more about street dance, courses are available through professional dance studios. Your local dance organization can also put you in touch with experienced teachers who can help you develop your skills.

Use the Internet or contact local dance organizations to find a good teacher and class near to you.

Top Tip

Studying different styles, such as jazz or contemporary dance, will make you a more versatile dancer, as well as giving you new ideas to incorporate into your street dance routines.

Programs and Classes

Most studios offer dance programs, as well as drop-in classes—before joining a program or class, you can ask to sit in and view a class to see if it is right for you. If you are interested in putting together your own routines, find out if the studio has a choreography group. This would give you the opportunity to learn more about street dance techniques, as well as the chance to help choreograph other dancers and perform to outside audiences.

Dancing as a Career

Being a professional dancer can be an amazing career. If you work with a touring company, it can give you the opportunity to travel the world. Most jobs are obtained through the audition process, where you compete against other dancers. You could also become a choreographer, a dance teacher, a commercial dancer in rock videos, movies, and TV, or a chorus-line dancer in **musical theater** productions. Dance is one of the biggest employers within the arts industry, employing hundreds of thousands of people in the U.S.A.

Professional dancers perform with some of the world's biggest pop stars. Here, two dancers accompany Kylie Minogue on stage during a live performance.

 Glossary

box step a dance move in which dancers step into the four corners of a square, creating a box-shaped pattern.

breaking a style of dance that evolved as part of hip-hop culture in the United States.

canon a group dance technique in which the dancers perform the same moves, one after the other.

choreography putting together sequences of movements, such as dance moves.

DJ an abbreviation of "disc jockey." In hip-hop music, a DJ selects, combines, and manipulates music recordings or small parts of songs.

electric boogaloo a dance style that combines popping with rolling hip, knee, and head movements.

freeze a technique in which the dancer moves the body and then suddenly halts, or freezes, all motion.

funk music a form of dance music based around a strong groove, or rhythm, typically supplied by drums and electric bass guitar.

hip-hop music a form of music based around the creation of beats by looping, or repeating, small, rhythmic portions of songs. It often features spoken or chanted rhyming lyrics.

isolation technique using muscle contractions to create quick, isolated movements.

jazz a musical style that originated in the southern United States, combining African and European music traditions.

locking The transition from a fast movement to a frozen moment where the body part is locked in a certain position.

mirroring a group dance technique in which dancers mirror each other's moves.

musical theater a form of theater that combines music, songs, spoken dialogue, and dance.

popping the quick contraction and relaxation of muscles to cause a jerk, or pop, in the dancer's body.

power moves a range of impressive floor-based street dance moves, featuring spins, rotations, and twirls.

R & B a contemporary musical style originally developed by African-American musicians, combining expressive vocal performances with hip-hop rhythms and jazz influences.

ripple a continuous movement of the body that uses isolation and rotation techniques to create a rippling effect.

rotation technique moving a body part in a rotating, isolated movement.

salsa a dance style based around the combination of Cuban and African rhythms.

tap a dance style based around the rhythmic tapping sound created by metal plates attached to the tap dancer's shoe.

unison technique where dancers perform identical movements in time with each other.

Dance Organizations

There are several organizations aimed at offering advice to street dancers. They can help you to find classes, apply for dance programs, and enter competitions.

Dance/USA is a national organization that provides help and support for individual dancers and dance companies throughout the United States.

The National Dance Education Organization (NDEO) works with federal and state agencies to promote high quality education in dance for children and adults.

The National Endowment for the Arts lists dance companies across the U.S.A. that provide educational and outreach programs as well as performances to inspire.

Further Reading

Street Jazz And Modern Dance
by Rita Storey (Sea To Sea Publications, 2007)

Street Dance: Set One
by Steve Rickard (Ransom Publishing, 2010)

The Best Dance Moves in the World... Ever!
by Matt Pagett (Chronicle Books, 2008)

Web Sites

Due to the changing nature of Internet links, PowerKids Press has developed an online list of Web sites related to the subject of this book. This site is updated regularly. Please use this link to access this list:
http://www.powerkidslinks.com/mt/dance/

Index